A Pretty Story

A Pretty Story

By

FRANCIS HOPKINSON
(Peter Grièvous [pseud.])

American Fiction Reprint Series

BOOKS FOR LIBRARIES PRESS
Freeport, New York

1969

First published in 1774 by John Dunlap (Philadelphia)

(Item #1230; Wright's AMERICAN FICTION 1774-1850)

Reprinted 1857 by Dana & Company (New York), under title
"The Old Farm and the New Farm: A Political Allegory"; with
an introduction and historical notes by Benson J. Lossing.

Reprinted 1969 in American Fiction Reprint Series
from the 1857 edition.

E211
H79
1969

STANDARD BOOK NUMBER:
8369-7004-7

LIBRARY OF CONGRESS CATALOG CARD NUMBER:
73-76925

PRINTED IN THE UNITED STATES OF AMERICA

THE

OLD FARM AND THE NEW FARM:

A Political Allegory.

BY

FRANCIS HOPKINSON,
MEMBER OF THE CONTINENTAL CONGRESS.

WITH

AN INTRODUCTION AND HISTORICAL NOTES

By BENSON J. LOSSING, M. A.,

AUTHOR OF "THE PICTORIAL FIELD-BOOK OF THE REVOLUTION,"
ETC., ETC.

NEW YORK:

DANA AND COMPANY,

381, BROADWAY.

1857.

Billin and Brother, *Stereotypers.*
Geo. Russell and Company, *Printers.*

DEDICATED

TO

THE YOUTH OF AMERICA,

AS

A RENEWAL OF GOOD SEED

ONCE PLANTED, SPRUNG UP, AND GROWN INTO A TREE,

WHOSE BRANCHES ARE

NUMEROUS AND WIDE-SPREADING.

This Story was written by a Revolutionary Patriot, more than eighty years ago. It tells, in a striking manner, of what then filled the minds and hearts of all Americans. It is plain English, common sense, and the honest truth. And now, while some of our countrymen are tempted to hint at a separation of the Union, it will do good to read here of old times, and to revive the spirit of the Continental Congress and of '76. Injustice led us to make common cause, and be the best of friends: and heart to heart, and shoulder to shoulder, E PLURI-BUS UNUM, we won our Independence, and laid the foundation of our prosperity. What was true then, is true now: UNITED WE STAND; DIVIDED WE FALL.

May all Americans, old and young, ever keep this in mind, and think, and feel, and speak, and act accordingly.

FRANCIS HOPKINSON.

INTRODUCTION.

THE political Allegory contained in the following pages, was written in the summer of 1774, by Francis Hopkinson, one of the signers of the Declaration of Independence. It was issued in a small pamphlet, by John Dunlap, in Philadelphia, early in September of that year, at the time when the first Continental Congress commenced its sessions in Carpenters' Hall, in that city. It was read with pleasure by the excited people throughout the colonies. The author was un-known, and even unsuspected, for a long time. It bore such evidence of genius, that several men, eminent for

1*

their learning and their patriotism, were suspected of its paternity.

Mr. Hopkinson was one of the brightest scholars and keenest wits of his day. He was a native of Philadelphia, where he was born on the 3d of September, 1738. His father was an English gentleman, of polished manners and a thorough education ; and his mother, a woman of great refinement, was the niece of the eminent Bishop of Worcester. They came from England immediately after their marriage, and settled in Philadelphia ; and there Mr. Hopkinson became active in public life, with Dr. Franklin and others. He was one of the founders of the College of Philadelphia.

When Francis was fourteen years of age, his father died, leaving a widow, with a large family of children. Francis was the first graduate of the new college, and was an honor to the institution. He chose the profession of law for a life vocation, and studied under Benjamin Chew, afterward the eminent Chief Justice of Pennsylvania. Being fond of literary pursuits, and feeling desirous to have his faculties expanded and strengthened by intercourse with eminent men, he went to England at the close of his law studies, and resided with the Bishop of Worcester about two years. Soon after his return, in 1768, he married Miss Ann Borden, the accomplished daughter of a wealthy gentleman, the founder of Bordentown, New Jersey. The colonies were then violently moved by political agitations, and his active mind often found expression through his pen. He wrote political essays for the newspapers, and several small pamphlets, the most attractive of which was the PRETTY STORY, contained in these pages. Like his conversation, it abounds with fine specimens of imagination, composition, and elegant wit. His language was ever remarkable for its great refinement; and he was never known to utter a profane word, nor an expression that would make a modest lady blush.

Mr. Hopkinson did not appear in public life until the Revolution had fairly commenced, when the colonies had drawn the sword, cast away the scabbard, and begun the War for Independence. Then he was chosen to represent New Jersey in the Continental Congress. A staunch patriot from the beginning, he never faltered in the onward march of the revolted colonies; and he heartily advocated and signed the Declaration of Independence. He was soon afterward commissioned a Judge of Admiralty for Pennsylvania, and while acting in that capacity, he wrote his witty and immortal poem. entitled *The Battle of the Kegs.*

When the Federal Constitution was before the people for consideration, Judge Hopkinson was one of its most zealous and eloquent supporters, with tongue and pen. In 1790, President Washington appointed him a Judge of the United States Court, for the district of Pennsylvania, under the new organization of the judiciary. He did not wear the ermine many months, for, on the 9th of May, 1791, he was suddenly smitten with epilepsy, which terminated his life in the course of a few hours.

The genius of Judge Hopkinson was versatile. He was a proficient in the knowledge of music, mathematics, mechanics, and chemistry. As a satirical writer he had few peers; and he was in the front rank of statesmen and jurists. His writings, arranged by himself, were published in three volumes, after his death, and are now exceedingly rare.

In annotating the PRETTY STORY, respect has been had to brevity and perspicuity. The explanations are hints or indices, rather than full information; yet they are quite sufficient to discover, at all times, the point of the Allegory, which contains, in brief outline, a history of the causes that kindled the old War for Independence. The reader will find it amusing and instructive.

B. J. L.

NEW YORK, *November*, 1856.

A

PRETTY STORY.

WRITTEN IN THE

Year of our LORD 1774,

BY

PETER GRIEVOUS, ESQ.,
A. B. C. D. E.

Veluti in Speculo.

PHILADELPHIA:
Printed and Sold by JOHN DUNLAP.
M,DCC,LXXIV.

AUTHOR'S PREFACE.

A BOOK *without a Preface is like a Face without a Nose. Let the other Features be ever so agreeable and well proportioned, it is looked on with Detestation and Horror if this material Ornament be wanting.*

Or rather, a Book is like a House: The grand Portico is the Dedication; the flagged Pavement is an humble Address to the Reader, in Order to pave the Way for a kind Reception of the Work; the Front Door with its fluted Pillars, Pediment, Trigliffs and Modillons are the Title Page with its Motto, Author's Name and Titles, Date of the Year, &c. The Entry is the Preface (oftentimes of a tedious Length) and the several Apartments and Closets are the Chapters and Sections of the Work itself.

As I am but a clumsy Carpenter at best, I shall not attempt to decorate my little Cottage with any out of Door Ornaments; but as it would be inconvenient and uncomfortable to have my Front Door open immediately into the Apartments of my House, I have made this Preface by Way of Entry.

And now, gentle Reader, if you should think my Entry too plain and simple you may set your Im-

*agination to work, and furnish it with a grand
Staircase, with Cornices, Stucco and Paintings.
That is, you may suppose that I entered very un-
willingly upon this Work, being compelled to it by a
Chain of unforeseen Circumstances: That it was
written in the Midst of a great Hurry of other Business, and under particular Disadvantages of Time
and Place, and that it was only intended for the
Inspection of a few Friends, without any Expecta-
tions of ever seeing it in the Press.*

*You may, kind Reader, go on to suppose that
when my Friends perused my Work, they were struck
with the Energy of my Genius, and insisted that the
Public ought not to be deprived of such a Fund of
Amusement and Improvement through my obstinate
Modesty; and that after many Solicitations and
powerful Persuasions I had been prevailed upon to
bless Mankind with the Fruits of my Labour.*

*Or, if you like not this, you may suppose that the
following Sheets were found in the Cabinet of some
deceased Gentleman; or that they were dug out of an
ancient Ruin, or discovered in a Hermit's Cave, or
dropped from the Clouds in a Hail Storm. In short
you may suppose just what you please. And when,
by the help of Imagination, you have seasoned the
Preface to your Palate, you may turn over this Leaf,
and feast upon the Body of the Work itself.*

THE NOBLEMAN GIVING THE GREAT PAPER TO HIS CHILDREN.

CHAPTER I.

ONCE upon a Time, a great While ago, there lived a certain Nobleman, who had long poffeffed a very valuable Farm, and had a great Number of Children and Grand-children.[1]

BESIDES the annual Profits of his Land, which were very confiderable, he kept a large Shop of Goods; and being very fuccefsful in

2

Trade, he became, in Procefs of Time, exceeding rich and powerful; infomuch that all his Neighbours feared and refpected him.[2]

WITH Refpect to the Management of his Family, it was thought he had adopted the moft perfect Mode that could be devifed, for he had been at the Pains to examine the Œconomy of all his Neighbours, and had felected from their Plans all fuch Parts as appeared to be equitable and beneficial, and omitted thofe which from Experience were found to be inconvenient. Or rather, by blending their feveral Conftitutions together he had fo ingenioufly counterbalanced the Evils of one Mode of Government with the Benefits of another, that the Advantages were richly enjoyed, and the Inconveniencies fcarcely felt. In fhort, his Family was thought to be the beft ordered of any in his Neighbourhood.[3]

HE never exercifed any undue Authority over his Children or Servants; neither indeed could he opprefs them if he was fo difpofed;

for it was particularly covenanted in his Marriage Articles[4] that he fhould not at any Time impofe any Tafks or Hardfhips whatever upon his Children without the free Confent of his Wife.[5]

Now the Cuftom in his Family was this, that at the End of every feven Years his Marriage became of Courfe null and void; at which Time his Children and Grandchildren met together and chofe another Wife for him, whom the old Gentleman was obliged to marry under the fame Articles and Reftrictions as before.[6] If his late Wife had conducted herfelf, during her feven Year's Marriage, with Mildnefs, Difcretion and Integrity, fhe was re-elected if otherwife, depofed :[7] By which Means the Children had always a great Intereft in their Mother in Law; and through her, a reafonable Check upon their Father's Temper. For befides that he could do nothing material refpecting his Children without her Approbation, fhe was fole Miftrefs of the Purfe Strings; and gave him out, from Time to Time, fuch Sums of Money as fhe thought neceffary for the Expences of his Family.[8]

BEING one Day in a very extraordinary good Humour, he gave his Children a Writing under his Hand and Seal, by which he releafed them from many Badges of Dependence, and confirmed to them feveral very important Privileges. The chief were the two following, viz., that none of his Children fhould be punifhed for any Offence, or fuppofed Offence, until his brethren had firft declared him worthy of fuch Punifhment;[9] and fecondly, he gave frefh Affurances that he would impofe no Hardfhips upon them without the Confent of their Mother in Law.[10]

This Writing, on account of its fingular Importance, was called THE GREAT PAPER.[11] After it was executed with the utmoft Solemnity, he caufed his Chaplain[12] to publish a dire Anathema againft all who fhould attempt to violate the Articles of the Great Paper, in the Words following.

* " In the Name of the Father, Son and
" Holy Ghost, AMEN! Whereas our Lord and
" Maſter, to the Honour of God and for the
" common Profit of this Farm hath granted,
" for him and his Heirs forever, theſe Articles
" above written : I, his Chaplain and ſpiritual
" Paſtor of all this Farm, do admoniſh the
" People of the Farm Once, Twice, and Thrice :
" Because that Shortneſs will not ſuffer ſo much
" Delay as to give Knowledge to the People of
" these Preſents in Writing ; I therefore enjoyn
" all Perſons, of what Eſtate ſoever they be, that
" they and every of them, as much as in them
" is, ſhall uphold and maintain theſe Articles
" granted by our Lord and Maſter in all Points.
" And all thoſe that in any Point do reſiſt, or
" break, or in any Manner hereafter procure,
" counſel or any Ways aſſent to reſiſt or break
" theſe Ordinances, or go about it by Word or
" Deed, openly or privately, by any Manner of

---

* This is a true and genuine Denunciation
copied from the Archives of the Family.
2*

" Pretence or Colour: I the aforefaid Chaplain,
"by my Authority, do excommunicate and ac-
"curfe, and from the Body of our Lord Jefus
"Chrift, and from all the Company of Heaven,
"and from all the Sacraments of the holy
"Church do fequefter and exclude."[13]

COMMENCING SETTLEMENTS.

CHAP. II.

NOW it came to pafs that this Nobleman
had, by fome Means or other, obtained a
Right to an immenfe Tract of wild unculti-
vated Country at a vaft Diftance from his Manfion Houfe.[1] But he fet little ftore by this Ac-
quifition, as it yielded him on Profit; nor was
it likely to do fo, being not only difficult of Accefs on Account of the Diftance, but was also
overrun with innumerable wild Beafts very

fierce and favage; fo that it would be ex-
tremely dangerous to attempt aking Poffeffion
of it.

IN Procefs of Time, however, fome of his
Children, more ftout and enterprifing than the
reft, requefted Leave of their Father to go and
fettle on this diftant Tract of Land.[2] Leave
was readily obtained; but before they fet out
certain Agreements were ftipulated between
them—the principal were—The old Gentleman,
on his Part, engaged to protect and defend the
Adventurers in their new Settlements; to affift
them in chacing away the wild Beafts, and to
extend to them all the Benefits of the Government under which they were born : Affuring
them that although they fhould be removed fo
far from his Prefence they fhould neverthelefs
be confidered as the Children of his Family,
and treated accordingly. At the fame Time
he gave each of them a Bond for the faith-
ful performance of thefe Promifes; in which,
among other Things, it was covenanted that
they fhould, each of them in their feveral Fam-

ilies, have a Liberty of making fuch Rules and
Regulations for their own good Government
as they fhould find convenient; provided thefe
Rules and Regulations fhould not contradict or
be inconfiftent with the general ftanding Orders
eftablifhed in his Farm.[3]

In Return for thefe Favours he infifted that
they, on their Parts, fhould at all Times acknowledge him to be their Father; that they
fhould not deal with their Neighbours without
his Leave, but fend to his Shop only for fuch
Merchandize as they fhould want.[4]   But in
Order to enable them to pay for fuch Goods as
they fhould purchafe, they were permitted to
fell the Produce of their Lands to certain of his
Neighbours.[5]

These Preliminaries being duly adjufted, our
Adventurers bid Adieu to the Comforts and
Conveniencies of their Father's Houfe, and fet
off on their Journey.[6]   Many and great were
the Difficulties they encountered on their Way:
but many more and much greater had they to

combat on their Arrival in the new Country.
Here they found Nothing but wild Nature.
Mountains over-grown with inacceffible Foliage,
and Plains fteeped in ftagnated Waters. Their
Ears are no longer attentive to the repeated
Strokes of induftrious Labour and the bufy
Hum of Men; inftead of thefe, the roaring
Tempeft and inceffant Howlings of Beafts of
Prey fill their minds with Horror and Difmay.
The needful Comforts of Life are no longer in
their Power—no friendly Roof to fhelter them
from inclement Skies; no Fortrefs to protect
them from furrounding Dangers. Unaccuf-
tomed as they were to Hardfhips like thefe,
fome were cut off by Sicknefs and Difeafe, and
others fnatched away by the Hands of Bar-
barity.[7]   They began, however, with great Per-
feverance, to clear the Land of encumbering
Rubbifh, and the Woods refound with the
Strokes of Labour; they drain the Waters
from the fedged Morafs, and pour the Sun
Beams on the reeking Soil; they are forced to
exercife all the powers of Induftry and Œconomy for bare Subfiftence, and like their firft

Parent, when driven from Paradiſe, to earn
their Bread with the Sweat of their Brows. In
this Work they were frequently interrupted by
the Incurſions of the wild Beaſts, againſt whom
they defended themſelves with heroic Proweſs
and Magnanimity.

After ſome Time, however, by Dint of in-
defatigable Perſeverance, they found themſelves
comfortably ſettled in this new Farm; and had
the delightful Proſpect of vast Tracts of Land
waving with luxuriant Harveſts, and perfuming
the Air with delicious Fruits, which before had
been a dreary Wilderneſs, unfit for the Habita-
tion of Men.[8]

In the mean Time they kept up a conſtant
Correſpondence with their Father's Family, and
at a great Expenſe provided Waggons, Horſes
and Drivers to bring from his Shop ſuch Goods
and Merchandize as they wanted, for which
they paid out of the Produce of their Lands.[9]

PAYING TRIBUTE TO THE NOBLEMAN'S WIFE.

CHAP. III.

NOW the new Settlers had adopted a Mode
of Government in their several Families
similar to that their Father had established in
the old Farm; in taking a new Wife at the
End of certain Periods of Time; which Wife
was chosen for them by their Children, and
without whose Consent they could do nothing
material in the Conduct of their Affairs.[1]   Under these Circumstances they thrived exceed-

ingly, and became very numerous; living in great Harmony amongſt themſelves, and in conſtitutional Obedience to their Father and his Wife.

Notwithstanding their ſuccefsful Progreſs, however, they were frequently annoyed by the wild Beaſts, which were not yet expelled the Country; and were moreover troubled by ſome of their Neighbours, who wanted to drive them off the Land, and take Poſſeſſion of it them-ſelves.[2]

To aſſiſt them in theſe Difficulties, and pro-tect them from Danger, the old Nobleman ſent over ſeveral of his Servants, who with the Help of the new Settlers drove away their Enemies. But then he required that they ſhould reim-burſe him for the Expence and Trouble he was at in their Behalf; this they did with great Cheerfulneſs, by applying from Time to Time to their reſpective Wives, who always com-manded their Caſh.[3]

Thus did Matters go on for a conſiderable
3

Time, to their mutual Happinefs and Benefit. But now the Nobleman's Wife began to caft an avaricious Eye upon the new Settlers; faying to herfelf, if by the natural Consequence of their Intercourfe with us my Wealth and Power are fo much increafed, how much more would they accumulate if I can perfuade them that all they have belonged to us, and therefore I may at any Time demand from them fuch Part of their Earnings as I pleafe.[4] At the fame Time fhe was fully fenfible of the Promifes and agreements her Hufband[5] had made when they left the old Farm, and of the Tenor and Purport of the Great Paper.[6] She therefore thought it neceffary to proceed with great Caution and Art, and endeavoured to gain her Point by imperceptible Steps.

IN Order to this, fhe firft iffued an Edict fetting forth, That whereas the Tailors of her Family were greatly injured by the People of the new Farm, inafmuch as they prefumed to make their own Clothes whereby the said Tailors were deprived of the Benefit of their

Cuſtom ; it was therefore ordained that for the future the new Settlers ſhould not be permitted to have amongſt them any Shears or Sciſſars larger than a certain fixed ſize. In Conſe-quence of this, our Adventurers were com-pelled to have their Clothes made by their Father's Tailors : But out of Regard to the old Gentleman, they patiently ſubmitted to this Grievance.[7]

ENCOURAGED by this Succeſs, ſhe proceeded in her Plan. Obſerving that the new Settlers were very fond of a particular Kind of Cyder which they purchaſed of a Neighbour, who was in Friendſhip with their Father (the Ap-ples proper for making this Cyder not growing on their own Farm) ſhe publiſhed another Edict, obliging them to pay her a certain Stipend for every Barrel of Cyder uſed in their Families ! To this likewiſe they ſubmitted : Not yet ſeeing the Scope of her Deſigns againſt them.[8]

AFTER this Manner ſhe proceeded, impoſing

Taxes upon them on various Pretences, and
receiving the Fruits of their Induftry with both
Hands. Moreover fhe perfuaded her Hufband
to fend amongft them from Time to Time a
Number of the moft lazy and ufelefs of his
Servants, under the fpecious Pretext of defend-
ing them in their Settlements, and of affifting
to deftroy the wild Beafts; but in Fact to rid
his own Houfe of their Company, not having
Employment for them; and at the fame Time
to be a Watch and a Check upon the People
of the new Farm.9

IT was likewife ordered that thefe Protectors.
as they were called, fhould be fupplied with
Bread and Butter cut in a particular Form:
But the Head of one of the Families refufed
to comply with this Order. He engaged to
give the Guefts, thus forced upon him, Bread
and Butter fufficient; but infifted that his
Wife fhould have the liberty of cutting it in
what fhape fhe pleafed.10

THIS put the old Nobleman into a violent

Paffion, infomuch that he had his Son's Wife
put into Gaol for prefuming to cut her Loaf
otherwife than as had been directed.[11]

3*

THE STEWARD LOOKING THE WIFE'S LIPS

CHAP. IV.

AS the old Gentleman advanced in Years he began to neglect the Affairs of his Family, leaving them chiefly to the Management of his Steward.[1] Now the Steward had debauched his Wife, and by that Means gained an entire Ascendency over her. She no longer deliberated what would moſt benefit either the old Farm or the new; but ſaid and did whatever the Steward pleaſed. Nay ſo much was fhe influenced by him that fhe could neither utter Ay or No but as he directed. For he had cunningly perfuaded her that it was very fafhionable for Women to wear Padlocks on their Lips, and that he was fure they would become her exceedingly. He therefore faftened a Padlock to each Corner of her Mouth; when the one was open, fhe could only fay Ay; and when the other was loofed, could only cry No. He took Care to keep the Keys of thefe Locks himfelf; fo that her Will became entirely fubject to his Power.[2]

Now the old Lady and the Steward had fet themfelves againft the People of the new Farm; and began to devife Ways and Means to impoverifh and diftrefs them.[3]

THEY prevailed on the Nobleman to fign an Edict againft the new Settlers, in which it was declared that it was their Duty as Children to pay fomething towards the fupplying their Father's Table with Provifions, and to the fupporting the Dignity of his Family; for that

Purpofe it was ordained that all their Spoons,
Knives and Forks, Plates and Porringers, fhould
be marked with a certain Mark, by Officers
appointed for that End; for which marking
they were to pay a certain Stipend : And that
they fhould not, under fevere Penalties, pre-
fume to make ufe of any Spoon, Knife or
Fork, Plate or Porringer, before it had been
fo marked, and the faid Stipend paid to the
Officer.[4]

THE Inhabitants of the new Farm began to
fee that their Father's Affections were alienated
from them; and that their Mother was but a
bafe Mother in Law debauched by their Enemy
the Steward. They were thrown into great
Confufion and Diftrefs. They wrote the moft
fupplicating Letters to the old Gentleman, in
which they acknowledged him to be their
Father in Terms of the greateft Refpect and
Affection—they recounted to him the Hardfhips and Difficulties they had fuffered in fet-
tling his new Farm; and pointed out the great
Addition of Wealth and Power his Family had

acquired by the Improvement of that Wilder-
nefs; and fhowed him that all the Fruits of
their Labours muft in the natural Courfe of
Things unite, in the long Run, in his Money
Box. They alfo, in humble Terms, reminded
him of his Promifes and Engagements on
their leaving Home, and of the Bonds he had
given them; of the Solemnity and Importance
of the Great Paper with the Curfe annexed.
They acknowledged that he ought to be reim-
burfed the Expences he was at on their Account, and that it was their Duty to affift in
fupporting the Dignity of his Family. All
this they declared they were ready and willing
to do; but requefted that they might do it
agreeable to the Purport of the Great Paper,
by applying to their feveral Wives for the
Keys of their Money Boxes and furnifhing
him from thence; and not be fubject to the
Tyranny and Caprice of an avaricious Mother
in Law, whom they had never chofen, and of a
Steward who was their declared Enemy.[5]

Some of thefe Letters were intercepted by

the Steward; others were delivered to the old
Gentleman, who was at the fame Time perfuaded to take no Notice of them; but, on
the Contrary, to infift the more ftrenuoufly
upon the Right his Wife claimed of marking
their Spoons, Knives and Forks, Plates and
Porringers.[6]

THE new Settlers, obferving how Matters
were conducted in their Father's Family became exceedingly diftreffed and mortified.
They met together and agreed one and all
that they would no longer fubmit to the arbitrary Impofitions of their Mother in Law,
and their Enemy the Steward. They determined to pay no Manner of Regard to the
new Decree, confidering it as a Violation of the
Great Paper. But to go on and eat their Broth
and Pudding as ufual. The Cooks alfo and
Butlers ferved up their Spoons, Knives and
Forks, Plates and Porringers, without having
them marked by the new Officers.[7]

THE Nobleman at length thought fit to re-

verfe the Order which had been made refpecting the Spoons, Knives and Forks, Plates and
Porringers of the new Settlers.[8] But he did
this with a very ill Grace: For he, at the fame
Time avowed and declared that he and his
Wife had a Right to mark all their Furniture,
if they pleafed, from the Silver Tankard down
to the very Chamber Pieces: That as he was
their Father he had an abfolute Controul over
them, and that their Liberties, Lives and Prop-
erties were at the entire Difpofal of him and
his Wife:[9] That it was not fit that he who
was allowed to be Omniprefent, Immortal, and
incapable of Error,[10] fhould be confined by the
Shackles of the Great Paper; or obliged to
fulfil the Bonds he had given them, which he
averred he had a Right to cancel whenever he
pleafed.[11]

His Wife alfo became intoxicated with
Vanity. The Steward had told her that fhe
was an omnipotent Goddefs, and ought to be
worfhipped as fuch: That it was the Height
of Impudence and Difobedience in the new

Settlers to difpute her Authority, which, with
Refpect to them, was unlimited : That as they
had removed from their Father's Family, they
had forfeited all Pretenfions to be confidered
as his Children, and loft the Privileges of the
Great Paper: That, therefore, fhe might look
on them only as Tenants at Will upon her
Hufband's Farm, and exact from them what
Rent fhe pleafed.[12]

ALL this was perfectly agreeable to Madam,
who admitted this new Doctrine in its full
Sense.[13]

THE People of the new Farm however took
little Notice of thefe pompous Declarations.
They were glad the marking Decree was re-
verfed, and were in Hopes that Things would
gradually fettle into their former Channel.[14]

SIGNING NON-IMPORTATION AGREEMENTS

CHAP. V.

IN the mean Time the new Settlers increaſed exceedingly, and as they increaſed, their Dealings at their Father's Shop were proportionably enlarged.[1]

IT is true they ſuffered ſome Inconveniencies from the Protectors that had been ſent amongſt them, who became very troubleſome in their Houſes: They ſeduced their Daughters; in-

4

troduced Riot and Intemperance into their
Families, and derided and infulted the Orders
and Regulations they had made for their own
good Government.[2] Moreover the old Nobleman had fent amongft them a great Number
of Thieves, Ravifhers and Murderers, who did
a great deal of Mifchief by practifing thofe
Crimes for which they had been banifhed the
old Farm.[3] But they bore thefe Grievances
with as much Patience as could be expected;
not choofing to trouble their aged Father with
Complaints, unlefs in Cafes of important Neceffity.

Now the Steward continued to hate the new
Settlers with exceeding great Hatred, and determined to renew his Attack upon their Peace
and Happinefs. He artfully infinuated to the
old Gentleman and his foolifh Wife, that it was
very mean and unbecoming in them to receive
the Contributions of the People of the new
Farm, towards fupporting the Dignity of his
Family, through the Hands of their respective
Wives: That upon this Footing it would be

in their Power to refuse his Requisitions whenever they should be thought to be unreasonable,
of which they would pretend to be Judges
themselves; and that it was high Time they
should be compelled to acknowledge his arbitrary Power, and his Wife's Omnipotence.

For this Purpose, another Decree was prepared and published, ordering that the new
Settlers should pay a certain Stipend upon particular Goods, which they were not allowed to
purchase any where but at their Father's Shop;
and that this Stipend should not be deemed an
Advance upon the original Price of the Goods,
but be paid on their arrival at the new Farm,
for the express Purpose of supporting the Dignity of the old Gentleman's Family, and of
defraying the Expences he affected to afford
them.[4]

THIS new Decree gave our Adventurers the
utmost Uneasiness. They saw that the Steward
and their Mother in Law were determined to
oppress and enslave them. They again met

together and wrote to their Father, as before, the moſt humble and perſuaſive Letters; but to little Purpoſe: A deaf Ear was turned to all their Remonſtrances; and their dutiful Requeſts treated with Contempt.[5]

FINDING this moderate and decent Conduct brought them no Relief, they had Recourſe to another Expedient. They bound themſelves in a ſolemn Engagement not to deal any more at their Father's Shop until this unconſtitutional Decree ſhould be reverſed; which they declared to be a Violation of the Great Paper.[6]

THIS Agreement was ſo ſtrictly adhered to, that in a few Months the Clerks and Apprentices in the old Gentleman's Shop began to make a ſad Outcry. They declared that their Maſter's Trade was declining exceedingly, and that his Wife and Steward would, by their miſchievious Machinations, ruin the whole Farm: They forthwith ſharpened their Pens and attacked the Steward, and even the old Lady herſelf with great Severity. Inſomuch that it was thought proper to withdraw this Attempt likewife upon the Rights and Liberties of the new Settlers. One Part only of the new De-cree remained unreverfed—viz. the Tax upon Water Gruel.[7]

Now there were certain Men on the old Farm, who had obtained from the Nobleman an exclufive Right of felling Water Gruel.[8] Vast Quantities of this Gruel were vended amongft the new Settlers; for it became very fafhionable for them to ufe it in their Families in great Abundance. They did not however trouble themfelves much about the Tax on Water Gruel: They were well pleafed with the Reverfal of the other Parts of the Decree, and confidering Gruel as not abfolutely necef-fary to the Comfort of Life, they were deter-mined to endeavour to do without it, and by that Means avoid the remaining effects of the new Decree.[9]

THE Steward found his Defigns once more fruftrated; but was not difcouraged by this Dif-

4*

appointment. He formed another Scheme fo artfully contrived that he thought himfelf fure of Succefs. He fent for the Perfons who had the fole Right of vending Water Gruel, and after reminding them of the Obligations they were under to the Nobleman and his Wife for their exclufive Privilege, he defired that they would fend fundry Waggon Loads of Gruel to the new Farm, promifing that the accuftomed Duty which they paid for their exclufive Right fhould be taken off from all the Gruel they fhould fend amongft the new Settlers: And that in Cafe their Cargoes fhould come to any Damage, he would take Care that the Lofs fhould be repaired out of the old Gentleman's Coffers.[10]

The Gruel Merchants readily confented to this Propofal, knowing that if their Cargoes were fold, they would reap confiderable Profits; and if they failed, the Steward was to make good the Damage. On the other hand the Steward concluded that the new Settlers could not refift purchafing the Gruel to which they had been fo long accuftomed; and if they did purchafe it when fubject to the Tax aforefaid, this would be an avowed acknowledgment on their Parts that their Father and his Wife had a Right to break through the Tenor of the Great Paper, and to lay on them what Impofi-tions they pleafed, without the Confent of their refpective Wives.[11]

But the new Settlers were well aware of this Decoy. They faw clearly that the Gruel was not fent to accommodate, but to enflave them; and that if they fuffered any Part of it to be fold amongft them, it would be deemed a Sub-miffion to the affumed Omnipotence of the Great Madam.[12]

DESTROYING THE WATER GRUEL CASKS.

CHAP. VI.

ON the Arrival of the Water Gruel, the People of the new Farm were again thrown into great Alarms and Confusions. Some of them would not suffer the Waggons to be un- loaded at all, but sent them immediately back to the Gruel Merchants: Others permitted the Waggons to unload, but would not touch the hateful Commodity; so that it lay neglected about their Roads and Highways until it grew

four and fpoiled.[1] But one of the new Settlers,
whofe Name was Jack,[2] either from a keener
Senfe of the Injuries attempted againft him, or
from the Neceffity of his Situation, which was
fuch that he could not fend back the Gruel becaufe of a Number of Mercenaries whom his
Father had ftationed before his Houfe to watch
and be a Check upon his Conduct: He, I fay,
being almoft driven to Defpair, fell to Work,
and with great Zeal ftove to Pieces the Cafks
of Gruel, which had been fent him, and utterly
demolifhed the whole Cargoe.[3]

These Proceedings were foon known at the
old Farm. Great and terrible was the uproar
there. The old Gentleman fell into great
Wrath, declaring that his abfent Children meant
to throw off all Dependence upon him, and to
become altogether difobedient. His Wife alfo
tore the Padlocks from her Lips, and raved and
ftormed like a Billingfgate. The Steward loft
all Patience and Moderation, fwearing moft
profanely that he would leave no Stone un-
turned 'till he had humbled the Settlers of the

new Farm at his Feet, and caufed their Father
to trample on their necks. Moreover the Gruel
Merchants roared and bellowed for the Lofs of
their Gruel; and the Clerks and Apprentices
were in the utmoft Confternation left the People
of the new Farm fhould again agree to have
no Dealings with their Father's Shop—Vengeance was immediately fet on Foot, particularly againft Jack. With him they determined
to begin; hoping that by making an Example
of him they fhould fo terrify the other Families
of the new Settlers, that they would all fubmit
to the Defigns of the Steward, and the Omnipotence of the old Lady.[4]

A very large Padlock was, accordingly, prepared to be faftened upon Jack's great gate;
the Key of which was to be given to the old
Gentleman; who was not to open it again until
he had paid for the Gruel he had fpilt, and re-
figned all Claim to the Privileges of the Great
Paper : Nor then neither unlefs he thought
fit.[5] Secondly, a Decree was made to new
model the Regulations and Œconomy of Jack's

Family in fuch Manner that they might for
the Future be more fubject to the Will of the
Steward.[6] And, thirdly, a large Gallows was
erected before the Manfion Houfe in the old
Farm, and an Order made that if any of Jack's
Children or Servants fhould be fufpected of
Mifbehaviour, they fhould not be convicted or
acquitted by the Confent of their Brethren,
agreeable to the Purport of the Great Paper,
but be tied Neck and Heels and dragged to
the Gallows at the Manfion Houfe, and there
be hanged without Mercy.[7]

No fooner did tidings of this undue Severity
reach the new Farm, but the People were almoft ready to defpair. They were altogether
at a Lofs how to act, or by what Means they
fhould avert the Vengeance to which they were
doomed : But the old Lady and Steward foon
determined the Matter ; for the Padlock was
fent over, and without Ceremony faftened upon
Jack's great Gate. They did not wait to know
whether he would pay for the Gruel or not, or
make the required Acknowledgments ; nor

give him the leaft Opportunity to make his
Defence—The great Gate was locked, and the
Key given to the old Nobleman, as had been
determined.[8]

POOR Jack found himfelf in a moft deplora-
ble Condition. The great Inlet to his Farm
was entirely blocked up, fo that he could
neither carry out the Produce of his Land for
Sale, nor receive from abroad the Neceffaries
for his Family.[9]

BUT this was not all—His Father, along with
the Padlock aforefaid, had fent an Overfeer to
hector and domineer over him and his Family;
and to endeavour to break his Spirit by exer-
cifing every poffible Severity: For which Purpofe he was attended by a great Number of
Mercenaries, and armed with more than common Authorities.[10]

ON his firft arrival in Jack's Family he was
received with confiderable Refpect, becaufe he
was the Delegate of their aged Father: For,

notwithftanding all that had paft, the People
of the new Settlements loved and revered the
old Gentleman with a truly filial Attachment;
attributing his unkindnefs entirely to the In-
trigues of their Enemy the Steward. But this
fair Weather did not laft long. The new
Overfeer took the firft Opportunity of fhowing
that he had no Intentions of living in Harmony
and Friendfhip with the Family. Some of
Jack's Domefticks had put on their Sunday
Clothes, and attended the Overfeer in the great
Parlour, in Order to pay him their Compli-
ments on his Arrival, and to requeft his Affift-
ance in reconciling them to their Father: But
he rudely ftopped them fhort, in the Midft of
their Speech; called them a Parcel of difobedient Scoundrels, and bid them go about their
Bufinefs. So faying, he turned upon his Heel,
and with great Contempt left the Room.[11]

5

HANDING SUPPLIES OVER THE GARDEN WALL

CHAP. VII.

NOW Jack and his Family finding themselves oppreſſed, inſulted and tyranniſed
over in the moſt cruel and arbitrary Manner,
adviſed with their Brethren what Meaſures
ſhould be adopted to relieve them from their
intolerable Grievances. Their Brethren, one
and all, united in ſympathiſing with their Af-
flictions; they adviſed them to bear their Suf-
ferings with Fortitude for a Time, aſſuring them

that they looked on the Punifhments and In-
fults laid upon them with the fame Indignation
as if they had been inflicted on themfelves, and
that they would ftand by and fupport them to
the laft. But, above all, earneftly recommended
it to them to be firm and fteady in the Cause of
Liberty and Juftice, and never acknowledge
the Omnipotence of their Mother in Law; nor
yield to the Machinations of their Enemy the
Steward.[1]

In the mean Time, left Jack's Family fhould
fuffer for Want of Neceffaries, their great Gate
being faft locked, liberal and very generous
Contributions were raifed among the feveral
Families of the new Settlements, for their
prefent Relief. This feafonable Bounty was
handed to Jack over the Garden Wall—All
Accefs to the Front of his Houfe being fhut
up.[2]

Now the Overfeer obferved that the Children
and Domefticks of Jack's Family had frequent
Meetings and Confultations together: Some-

times in the Garret, and fometimes in the Stable : Underftanding, likewife, that an Agreement not to deal in their Father's Shop, until
their Grievances fhould be redreffed, was much
talked of amongft them, he wrote a thundering
Prohibition, much like a Pope's Bull,[3] which
he caufed to be pafted up in every Room in
the Houfe : In which he declared and protefted
that thefe Meetings were treafonable, traiterous
and rebellious ; contrary to the Dignity of their
Father, and inconfiftent with the Omnipotence
of their Mother in Law : Denouncing alfo
terrible Punifhments againft any two of the
Family who fhould from thenceforth be feen
whifpering together, and ftrictly forbidding the
Domefticks to hold any more Meetings in the
Garret or Stable.[4]

THESE harfh and unconftitutional Proceedings irritated Jack and the other inhabitants of
the new Farm to fuch a Degree that * * * * *

Cœtera defunt.[5]

EDITOR'S NOTES.

CHAPTER I.

[1] The *Nobleman* is the king of Great Britain; the *valuable farm* is his kingdom, and his *children and grand children* are his subjects.

[2] When Agricola, in the year of our Lord, 85, completed the Roman conquest of Britain, the people were semi-barbarians, and for more than a thousand years they made very little progress in commerce. It was not until it had flourished a long time in the countries bordering on the Mediterranean Sea, that the English people discovered its value. When, at length, they engaged in it, they prosecuted it with energy, soon outstripped their continental neighbors, and by its means they acquired both enormous wealth and immense political power. The British nation is yet the chief power in Europe, respected alike for its moral and intellectual greatness, and for its material strength.

[3] The British Constitution is an abstract of the collective wisdom of many generations in the science of government. The foundation of the common law of England, is the code

5*

of Alfred, compiled chiefly from existing laws, in the year
1065. Stephen gave the people a charter of general liberties
in 1136, and this was confirmed by Henry the Second in
1154 and 1175. New laws have been incorporated with the
old, from time to time; and for about a thousand years the
people of Great Britain have had rights and privileges in-
alienable. These were promulgated by the Great Charter
given in 1215 and confirmed in 1216. The British Constitution is the *perfect mode* here referred to.

⁴ The necessary acts of Parliament which determine the
succession to the throne, and the solemn covenants entered
into between the sovereign and the people, at the coronation,
are the *marriage articles* here mentioned.

⁵ The *wife* of the Nobleman is the British Parliament, to
which the sovereign is amenable in acts and person. The
word is from the French *Parler la ment,*—to speak one's
mind,—and indicates the right of the members of that assembly to speak freely upon all matters relating to the common-
wealth. This title was given after the Norman conquest of
Britain, in the year 1066. The Saxons called it *Witenage
Mote,*—that is, the Great *Mote*, meeting or Assembly. Parliament possesses supreme power in making and repealing
laws, and in all acts pertaining to the government of the
realm. It is composed of the hereditary House of Lords,
and the elective House of Commons. The government ex-
hibits three estates, so called, namely, King, Lords and
Commons.

⁶ Members of the House of Commons are elected every
seven years; and when the newly chosen members take their

seats, they utter a solemn oath to support the British Constitution. This is the Marriage with the King. In 1694, the period of each parliament's duration was fixed at three years. In 1716, the "Septennial Act" was passed, and the "Triennial Act" of 1694 was repealed. Since then there has been no change. The "Chartists" of our day demand annual parliaments. Under the "Septennial Act" of 1716, the sovereign has power to shorten the duration of parliament, by dissolution. Because the parliament, elected in 1830, declined to pass the first reform bill, William the Fourth dissolved it in April, 1831.

[7] The people, at their elections, may choose new representatives, if they please, or may re-elect the old ones. In this way the *Wife* may be retained or deposed, at the end of seven years.

[8] The Sovereign has no power to levy taxes, without the consent of Parliament. Nor can he compel men to serve in civil or military capacities, by his own will. As early as the reign of Edward the First, this matter was settled by a special act of Parliament. Edward commanded some of his nobles to serve in an expedition against the French King. The Earl Marshal of his realm refused obedience, unless the King would go in person. "You shall go without me," said Edward. The Earl replied, "I am not so bound, and will not take that journey without you." The King, in a rage, swore that he should "either go or hang." "And I swear," said the Earl, "that I will neither go nor hang." And he did not. Parliament soon afterward passed the act called *De Tallagio non concidendo*, which affirms the absolute power of that body in providing money, men, and other things for

the public use. The usurpation of this power by the Sovereign, at different times, has produced popular commotions. It cost Charles the First his head.

· ⁹ This refers to Trial by Jury. It was known as early as the Saxon Heptarchy, or the government of England by seven kings, formed in the year 455. It was incorporated into Alfred's code, and is considered as the great bulwark of the people's liberty.

¹⁰ The Supremacy of Parliament, mentioned in Note 8.

¹¹ The "Great Paper," is the Magna Charta or Great Charter of English liberties, which was extorted from King John by a large number of Barons. It was a body of laws already in use, the letter and spirit of which had been grossly violated by John. The Barons took arms to enforce this sacred possession, and John reluctantly signed the Great Charter, at Runnymede, near Windsor, in June, 1215. In this act the supreme power of Parliament was acknowledged, for the Charter was submitted to that body for confirmation. (See the picture at the head of this chapter.)

¹² Robert, Archbishop of Canterbury, was then the Primate, or Chief Ecclesiastic of England.

¹³ This was put forth in 1216, at the command of Henry the Third. It was ordered that the Charter should be read by all Archbishops and Bishops, in the cathedral churches, twice a year, and "upon reading thereof in every of their parish churches," they were openly to denounce, by this oath, all that should do any thing contrary to the letter and spirit of the Charter.

CHAPTER II.

¹ The British possessions, by right of discovery, in North America, are here meant.

² This refers to the various individuals and companies who obtained Charters from the King for making settlements in America.

³ In all the Charters it was covenanted expressly or by implication, that while the settlers should enjoy all the rights guaranteed by the Great Charter, they were to acknowledge the supremacy of the King and Parliament, and be governed by British laws.

⁴ From the first, the British Government coveted the monopoly of all the gain that might be derived from settlements in the New World. Specifications for that purpose were made in the Charters. And afterward, when the colonies began to flourish and germs of commerce appeared, the parent government unwisely attempted to control their trade, and make it subservient to the gain of the people of Great Britain. Out of restrictions imposed upon the industry of the colonies, by successive Acts of Parliament, grew much ill-feeling.

⁵ The colonists were allowed to export some of their products to the French, Spanish, Portuguese and Dutch West Indies.

⁶ The various expeditions for the purpose of settlements in America, are here alluded to.

⁷ The first adventurers suffered severely from disease, privations, and often from the hostilities of the Indians. One half of the first emigrants to Virginia, in 1607, perished in the course of a few weeks. Of five hundred left by Smith, in Virginia, in 1609, only sixty remained at the end of six months. A little later, three hundred and fifty white people were massacred by the Indians, within an hour ; and in the course of a few days, eighty plantations were reduced to eight. Within a little more than three months, forty of the one hundred people who landed at Plymouth in 1620, were in their graves. These illustrations might be multiplied.

⁸ Within the period of a little more than a century, flourishing English colonies were making the wilderness blossom like a garden, all along the Atlantic from the St. Croix in the north-east, to the St. Mary's in the south, a distance of more than a thousand miles.

⁹ Feeble commercial efforts were made early in New England. In 1636, a vessel of thirty tons made a voyage from thence to the West Indies ; and not long afterward American vessels were seen in the ports of Great Britain.

CHAPTER III.

¹ These wives were the Colonial Legislatures. The several Colonial Governments were modelled after that of Great Britain, and their laws were all made in conformity to the British Constitution. The right to dissolve these Legislatures rested in the Royal Governors, in imitation of the right of the King to dissolve Parliament.

² The wild beasts were the Indians, and their neighbors were the French in Canada and the Spaniards in Florida.

³ British troops were sent over, at various periods, to assist the colonists against their neighbors on the north and south, and the Indians all around them. The expenses of expeditions got up for the purpose were generally paid by the resp...tive colonies, taxes for raising the money being levied by the "wives,"—the Colonial Assemblies,—and of course cheerfully paid by the people. At one time during the French and Indian war, the people of Massachusetts paid a tax on real estate, equal, in many instances, to two-thirds of the income of the tax-payer. In Massachusetts alone, at that time, public and private advances, for the common good, amounted to more than a million of dollars.

⁴ The assumption, theoretically and practically, of the right of the British Government to tax the colonies without their consent was the chief cause which produced the war for Independence. The colonies had no representatives in the Imperial Parliament, and they planted the foot of opposition upon the firm political postulate, that TAXATION, WITHOUT REPRESENTATION, IS TYRANNY.

⁵ The King, in whose name all covenants are made.

⁶ Magna Charta.

⁷ This refers to the various restrictions imposed upon the industry of the colonists, from time to time, by Acts of Parliament. The Navigation Act of 1651, forbade all importations into England except in English ships, or those belonging to English colonies. Another Act, in 1660, forbade

the colonists sending any sugar, tobacco, pitch, and other
American productions, into any port of Europe except of the
dominions of England. Early in the eighteenth century,
domestic manufactures had greatly increased among the
colonists, and quite a profitable intercolonial trade was in
progress. The cupidity of the English Government sought
to repress these industrial operations. The exportation of
hats and other commodities from one colony to another was
prohibited. All manufactories of iron and steel were pro-
nounced "nuisances" to be immediately abated; hatters
were allowed to have only two apprentices at one time, and
the Carolinians were forbidden to cut down the pine trees
of their vast forests and convert their wood into staves and
their juices into turpentine and tar. Brigantines and small
sloops had commenced voyages from Massachusetts and
Pennsylvania, to exchange the products of those provinces
for rum, sugar, wine, and silks, with the West India merchants. To repress this commerce, the importation into the
colonies of those West India productions were burdened with
exorbitant duties. And thus, in many ways, Great Britain
sought to compel the colonists to trade only with its people;
to pursue agriculture, and to purchase what they needed of
British manufacturers. The colonies became very good customers. From 1738 to 1748, the average value of exports
from Great Britain to the American colonies, was almost
three and a quarter millions of dollars annually.

 [8] Heavy duties were laid upon rum imported from the
West Indies, and upon wines from other countries. These
composed the *cider* alluded to. At about the same time,
(1763,) the Earl of Bute, George the Third's first prime minister, imposed a heavy tax upon cider used in England, to be

paid by the first purchaser. It produced much excitement and opposition. The amount of tax was reduced, and the payment shifted to the shoulders of the producer. This did not alter the case as a grievance, and many who had orchards, declared they would let their apples rot on the trees, before they would make them into cider, under such excise regulations. There had not been such excitement in England since the famous tax measures of Sir Robert Walpole thirty years before.

[9] At the conclusion of the French and Indian war in 1763, quite a great number of British troops were left in America, and others were sent over from time to time, ostensibly to assist in keeping the French and Indians at bay, but really to enforce revenue laws and to repress the democratic principle, everywhere manifested. The imperial treasury had been completely exhausted by the late war, and ministers had resolved to replenish it in part by indirectly taxing the colonies. The troops were to be instrumental in accomplishing the measure. Much ill feeling was produced, and in the Declaration of Independence it was alleged as a serious charge against the King, that "He has kept among us, in times of peace, standing armies, without the consent of our Legislatures."

[10] The colonists were required to make partial provision for the troops quartered among them. New York and Massachusetts refused to give them food and shelter. Parliament then passed the Mutiny Act, as it was called, which provided that British troops sent hither, should be provided, by the colonists, with quarters, beer, salt, and vinegar. These stipu-

lations were the orders for cutting the bread and butter in a particular form.

 " The Assembly of New York was the *head of one of the families,* who refused compliance. The Act empowered any officer, on obtaining a warrant, to enter any house in search of deserters. This privilege might be greatly abused, and the Briton's boast that "every man's house is his castle," not to be violated, would no longer be tenable. The Assembly steadily refused to make provision for the troops, and as a punishment for this contumacy, Parliament, in 1767, passed an act, "prohibiting the Governor, Council and Assembly of New York passing any legislative act, for any purpose whatever." This was putting *the son's wife into gaol* for presuming to cut her loaf otherwise than she had been directed.

CHAPTER IV.

[1] The Prime Minister and his associates, who wield a great power in the government.

[2] On the accession of George the Third, and for many years afterward, the King and Parliament were completely controlled by the Ministry. They originated all governmental schemes, and the elected representatives of the people, with a few exceptions, seemed to have all the thinking done for them, while they went through the formality of a vote, only to give legality to ministerial measures. They seemed to have the privilege of only saying *Aye* and *No*, as the Ministry directed.

[3] The colonists were flourishing, and the British treasury

was empty, at the commencement of the reign of George the Third. These appeared sufficient reasons for taxing the colonists. They were willing to be taxed, but only by their own Assemblies. The pride of the Ministry and Parliament would not allow this, and for more than ten years, or until the breaking out of the war for independence, in 1775, the British government, blind to justice and its own interests, seemed intent upon distressing the Americans.

⁴ This is in allusion to the famous "Stamp Act" of 1765, which declared that no legal instrument of writing should be valid in the colonies, unless it bore a government stamp, for which a specific sum had been paid. These stamps were upon blue paper, bearing the British arms and an impression of the price. These were to be affixed to the various instruments of writing, and promised to produce quite a large income. But the Americans, perceiving it to be taxation in another form, resolved not to submit. The "Stamp Act" became a law by receiving the signature of the King in the Spring of 1765.

⁵ The passage of the "Stamp Act" produced great excitement in the colonies. The people saw in it real oppression, and they resolved to meet and discuss the matter. Delegates, appointed in several colonies, met in the city of New York in October 1765, less than a month before the law was to go into effect. They continued in session fourteen days, and in three well-written documents they expressed their loyalty, and their willingness to be taxed by their own Legislatures; set forth their grievances; asserted their rights under the British Constitution, and petitioned the King and Parliament for justice. They confidently appealed to the Constitution,—

the Great Paper,—and while they declared their loyalty they claimed their constitutional privileges, with sturdy pertinacity.

⁶ George the Third was a weak but not a wicked man. He was sometimes obstinate, but, lacking the qualifications of a statesman, he (unwisely for himself) yielded his own opinions to those of his chosen advisers. These, perhaps both blind and wicked, resolved to enforce the "Stamp Act," with all the power of the government. They asserted the supremacy of Parliament; and the King, though kindly disposed towards his American subjects, was persuaded to acquiesce in coercive measures.

⁷ The Americans were firm. The proceedings of the Stamp Act Congress were applauded by all of the Colonial Assemblies in defiance of the frowns of the royal governors; and the people of America were as firmly united, in heart and purpose, then, as they were after the Declaration of Independence more than ten years later. The first of November, when the act was to go into effect, was observed as a day of fasting and mourning. There were funeral processions and bells tolling funeral knells. The courts were closed, all business was suspended, and gloom prevailed. The lull in the storm was brief. The great heart of the public, just now so quiet, suddenly palpitated with full force, aroused by firm and spontaneous resolves to be free. Rebellion was in every heart, and dwelt on many a lip. Mobs assailed the dwellings of officials; merchants entered into agreements not to import any more goods from Great Britain while that act was a law, and domestic manufactures were commenced in every family, the wealthy vying with the middling classes in self-denial. Soon a respectful but firm

protest went over the Atlantic to the ears of the British ministry,—the wicked *Steward*,—and it was seconded there by the merchants and manufacturers, whose American trade was prostrated. The voice, thus made potential, was heard and heeded in high places, while the Americans, conscious of right, utterly disregarded the act, and *ate their broth and pudding as usual.*

[8] Ministers became alarmed and found it expedient to retrace their steps. William Pitt, England's greatest Commoner, was now in Parliament as a champion of the American people. Edmund Burke was also there, on the same side, and now first astonished the public by his brilliant oratory in his advocacy of the rights of the Americans. They both earnestly urged the repeal of the Stamp Act, and in March, 1766, that measure was effected, to the great joy of the business men of Great Britain, and the whole of the American people.

[9] Jealous of the honor of Great Britain, and doubtful of the passage of the repeal act without a salvo for that honor, Pitt appended to it an act which declared that Parliament possessed the power "to bind the colonies in all cases whatsoever." After the excess of their joy had abated, the colonists perceived in this Declaratory Act, an egg of tyranny, and were both incensed and alarmed. They perceived that Parliament had conceded nothing of its high assumption, and they naturally anticipated the development of other schemes to enslave them.

[10] The King can never die, and the King can do no wrong, have ever been maxims of British law. The first is based upon the fact that the throne is always filled; and the latter

6*

upon the assumption that so excellent a person as the King ought to be, will not do wrong, and also that he does nothing without his ministers.

[11] The British Sovereign has sometimes been bold enough to assert, by implication at least, like the French King, " I am the State;" but thus far Magna Charta and the Parliament have controlled the throne, and always will.

[12] Such doctrines were put forth by Lord North, who misgoverned Great Britain during the whole of our war for independence. He was a zealous advocate of the omnipotence of Parliament, whether its decrees were right or wrong; and long before the good King could be persuaded to speak of the Americans as rebels, North had boldly proclaimed them such. He regarded them as out of the pale of British protection, because they had dared to question the justice of British rule; and he was disposed to treat them as tenants at will.

[13] Parliament, by its votes on subjects respecting its omnipotence, exhibited its perfect agreement with the Prime Minister.

[14] Encouraged by the success of their firmness in opposing the Stamp Act, the Americans paid very little attention to the Declaratory Act, and they pressed forward in the path of their prosperity until ministers commenced working the engine of oppression, anew.

CHAPTER V.

[1] For several months after the repeal of the Stamp Act, the Americans enjoyed the repose born of fond hope of justice in the future. They renewed their trade with Great Britain, and all ill feeling subsided.

[2] In many ways the troops quartered among the people were a very great annoyance. They were licentious, set bad examples for the young men, and by their insolence kept alive the hatred of the people, and fanned the flame of rebellion.

[3] New and unnecessary offices were created, and bad men, who left their country for their country's good, often, were appointed to fill them. Among others came insolent Commissioners of Customs, who mistook the temper of the people, and greatly increased the public irritation.

[4] Soon after fresh troops were sent to America to enforce obnoxious laws, new taxation schemes were laid before Parliament, by the Ministry. In June, 1767, a duty was levied upon tea, glass, painters' colors, etc., imported into the colonies ; and in July another bill, establishing a Board of Trade in the colonies independent of colonial legislation, and creating resident Commissioners of Customs, to enforce the revenue laws, was passed. Then came another for punishing the contumacious New York Assembly.

[5] Again the greatest excitement prevailed throughout the colonies. The Colonial Assemblies boldly protested. Peti-

tions to the King, and remonstrances to Parliament, were
sent. Pamphlets and newspapers were filled with inflam-
matory appeals, defining the rights of the people as British
subjects, and urging them to united resistance of these direct
blows at popular liberty. Early in 1768, almost every Colonial
Assembly had expressed the opinion that Parliament had no
right to tax the Americans without their consent. The Ministry, blind and wicked still, turned a deaf ear to petitions
and remonstrances, and treated the most respectful words
with utter contempt.

⁶ Non-importation leagues, so powerful against the Stamp
Act, were now renewed.

⁷ The refusal of the colonies to import from Great Britain,
again bore heavily upon the British merchants and manufacturers, for the Americans had become their most important
customers. Again there was a loud clamor raised against the
Ministry and the majority in Parliament, and after a strug-
gle for almost three years, the Ministry and their supporters were compelled to yield. The duty upon all but tea,
was taken off, and that was retained merely to assert the
right of Parliament to levy such duty. This was the *Water
Gruel.*

⁸ These were the members of the English East India Company. That association was formed and chartered in the
year 1600, for the purpose of carrying on a trade between
England and the countries lying east of the Cape of Good
Hope. It was this company, when it had become rich, and
very powerful in the East, that gave to Great Britain the
foundation of its mighty empire in the East Indies, which
now comprises the whole of Hindostan from Cape Comorin

to the Himalaya Mountains, with a population of more than one hundred and twenty millions of souls. This company was a vast monopoly, and had the exclusive right of selling tea.

⁹ The colonists, feeling that they could very well dispense with the luxury of tea, entered generally into leagues not to use it. It was a small privation for the consumers, but the East India Company felt the loss of their customers here, severely.

¹⁰ Early in 1773, a new thought upon taxation entered the brain of Lord North. The East India Company had then more than seventeen millions of pounds of tea in their London warehouses, and feeling the loss of their American customers, they petitioned Parliament to take off the import duty of three pence per pound upon all sent to America. The company agreed to pay more than an equal amount, in export duty, to the government. Here was a good opportunity for the government to be just, wise, and conciliatory. The stupid ministry refused, because it might be considered submission to "rebellious subjects ;" and misapprehending the real question at issue, North introduced a bill into Parliament, allowing the company to send their tea free of export duty, supposing the Americans would purchase it at the cheaper rates. This concession to a commercial monopoly, while spurning the just appeals of a great people, moved by a noble principle, only created contempt and indignation throughout the colonies.

¹¹ The East India Company, as blind as Ministers, regarded the American market as now open for their tea, and soon after the passage of the bill, in May, 1773, several large ships,

laden with the obnoxious plant, were on their way across the Atlantic.

[12] Intelligence of the new movement reached America before the arrival of any of the tea ships. The people saw clearly that submission to this almost nominal tax, was as much an acknowledgment of the assumed right of Parliament to levy it as if it was tenfold greater, and they resolved to resist the tyranny in every form.

CHAPTER VI.

[1] In most of the seaboard towns where consignments of tea had been made, the people resolved, at public meetings, that it should not even be landed. The ships which arrived at New York and Philadelphia were sent back to England with their cargoes. At Charleston it was landed, but was not allowed to be sold; and at Annapolis quite a great quantity was destroyed.

[2] Massachusetts is here called *Jack.*

[3] The people of Boston held several meetings, warned the consignees that the tea should not be landed, and prepared for prompt action on its arrival. These meetings were led by the best men in Boston. Two vessels came, and were moored at Griffin's wharf. On the afternoon of December 16, 1773, a large meeting upon the subject was held in Faneuil Hall. It was now ascertained that Governor Hutchinson and his friends had resolved that the tea should be landed, in defiance of the public feeling. Twilight approached, and candles

were about to be lighted, when one or two persons in the gallery, disguised as Mohawk Indians, gave a war-whoop. It was answered from without. The Assembly was immediately broken up, and a large number of persons rushed toward the wharf where the tea-ships were moored. About sixty persons, some of them in Indian disguise, boarded the vessels, tore open the hatches, and in the course of two hours, three hundred and forty-two chests, containing the proscribed article, were broken open, and their contents cast into the waters of Boston harbor. The *Mercenaries* alluded to in the text, were the Governor and numerous officials, who resided in Boston.

⁴ The destruction of the tea at Boston produced a powerful sensation throughout the British realm. While the American colonies, and even Canada, Nova Scotia, and the West Indies, sympathized with the Bostonians and could not censure them, the exasperated government adopted retaliatory measures, notwithstanding a promise was given to the East India Company, that full payment should be made for all losses they sustained. The ministerial party in Parliament were very violent in their denunciations; and one member, after declaring that the people of Boston "ought to have their town knocked about their ears," uttered the sentiment of the old Roman orators when they wished to excite the people against the Carthagenians,—"Delenda est Carthago,"—*Carthage must be destroyed.*"

⁵ Parliament, by enactment, on the 7th of March, 1774, ordered the port of Boston to be closed against all commercial transactions whatever, and the removal of the customhouse, courts of justice, and other offices, to Salem. This was the *padlock on Jack's gate.* The act, known as the

Boston Port Bill, also provided, that when the Bostonians should fully submit, the King should have power to open the port.

⁶ Soon after the passage of the Port Bill, another act was passed for "better regulating the Government of Massachusetts Bay." It was equivalent to a total subversion of the ancient charter, inasmuch as it took from the people, and placed in the hands of the governor, the nomination of all military, executive, and judicial officers, and gave to the crown the appointment of counsellors and judges of the Supreme Court.

⁷ On the 21st of April, 1774, another retaliatory act was passed. It provided for the trial in England of persons in the service of the crown, in the colonies, who might be charged with murder, thus taking the matter from colonial juries. This was denounced in Parliament, as "encouragement to military insolence already so insupportable." At tne same time provision was made for conveying to England, for trial and punishment, such persons in the Massachusetts colony as should be charged with treason to the government. This was denounced as tyranny, and unconstitutional to the last degree. Earlier than this [1769] Parliament, by resolution, prayed the King to revive a long obsolete statute of Henry the Eighth, by which the governor of any colony might arrest, and send to England for trial, any person charged with treason.

⁸ When the news of these oppressive measures reached America, the people were exceedingly indignant. Boston was clearly doomed to destruction. The inhabitants of Salem patriotically refused the privilege of having the custom

house and courts of justice there; and those of Marblehead, fifteen miles distant, offered the free use of their harbor and wharves to the merchants of Boston. The padlock came. On the first of June, 1774, the Boston Port Bill went into operation, and all business was suspended in the doomed city. Jack's gate was locked.

⁹ The inhabitants of Boston were in a very unhappy condition. Martial law prevailed. General Gage, then the royal ruler there, resolved to stop all intercourse between the city and country; and fearing the indignation of the people, he commenced fortifying the neck of land which connects Boston with the main. There was a complete embargo, and distress prevailed in the city.

¹⁰ For the avowed purpose of enforcing the oppressive laws, General Gage, the commander-in-chief of the British army in America, was appointed Governor of Massachusetts; and at the time specified for the Port Bill to go into operation, he had quite a great number of troops in Boston.

¹¹ Gage went to Boston attended only by his staff. A large concourse of people received him with respect, for they were unwilling to prejudge him; and, moreover, he was the representative of the King, toward whom, in the midst of all their excitement, the colonists felt and expressed the warmest loyalty. Few, at that time, entertained an idea of political independence of Great Britain. The magistrates and others entertained the General at a public dinner, and that night an effigy of the obnoxious Governor Hutchinson was burned in front of John Hancock's mansion. But Gage was commissioned to execute harsh measures, and he at once informed the people that he should carry out the commands of Parlia-

7

ment to the fullest extent. He soon became an odious tyrant in the eyes of the inhabitants, for he turned from them with contempt and threatened them with punishment for insolence.

CHAPTER VII.

[1] The people of Boston suffered terribly, yet they were firm. They received encouragement, sympathy, and substantial aid, from all quarters. The Colonial Assemblies exhorted them to perseverance, and the people, in primary assemblages, conjured them not to falter in their opposition to the monstrous assumptions of Parliament.

[2] Grain, provisions, money, and clothing, were sent to the people of Boston, from every province; and the city of London, in its corporate capacity, subscribed one hundred and fifty thousand dollars in aid of the suffering inhabitants of the doomed town.

[3] This is the title of Special Edicts issued by the Pope of Rome. They are written on parchment, and have a great seal attached, made of wax, lead, silver, or gold. The name is derived from the seal, *bulla*. On one side are the heads of Peter and Paul, and on the other the name of the reigning Pope, and the year of his pontificate. The seal of the celebrated *Golden Bull* of the Emperor Charles the Fourth was made of gold. That Bull became the fundamental law of the German Empire, at the Diet of Nuremberg, A. D. 1536.

[4] The patriot leaders were not dismayed. On the day after the arrival of Gage, a large meeting was held in Faneuil Hall,

over which Samuel Adams presided. From it went forth, to all the colonies, a proposition to relinquish all intercourse with Great Britain until the Port Bill should be repealed. And when Gage had transferred the government offices to Salem, and called a meeting of the General Court, or Legislature, there, the opposition leaders held various meetings to consult upon a course of action. When the General Court opened, the various measures they had matured were boldly laid before that body. On being informed of these proceedings, Gage sent his Secretary to dissolve the Assembly, but he found the door locked, and the key was in Samuel Adams's pocket. The patriots then signed a non-importation league, and appointed a committee to send a copy to all the Colonial Assemblies, with a recommendation to adopt it. Gage was irritated by their boldness, and issued a strong proclamation, denouncing the proceedings of the Assembly as seditious, and ordering the magistrates to apprehend and bring to trial all who should sign it. He also forbade all secret meetings, or public assemblies. This proclamation was posted everywhere, but the people laughed at it, defied the pliant magistrates, and signed the league by thousands. The press, on the side of freedom, was equally bold, and Gage was burlesqued. As a specimen of the manner in which the patriots bearded the lion, the following extract from a published poetical paraphrase of one of Gage's proclamations, is given:

> " Tom Gage's Proclamation,
>   Or blustering Demonstration,
>   (Replete with Defamation)
>   Threatening Devastation
>   And speedy Jugulation
>   Of the New English Nation,
>   Who shall his pious ways **shun.**

Thus graciously the war I wage,
As witnesseth my hand,—

TOM GAGE.

" By command of Mother Carey,
THOMAS FLUCKER, Secretary."

It may interest the reader to know that General Henry
Knox, the commander of the artillery during the Revolution,
married Lucy, daughter of Thomas Flucker.

⁵ "The rest is wanting." Here, upon the threshold of the
that great Revolution which resulted in the independence of
thirteen British colonies in America, the writer closed his
allegory. The PRETTY STORY ended just as the GREAT DRAMA
commenced. The author had then seen only the gradual
uplifting of the curtain; and he little suspected that he
should become one of the chief actors in the momentous
scenes of that drama. It closed brilliantly. A great nation
was born; and to-day the Wife (Congress) of the Son is
as potent as the Wife (Parliament) of the old Nobleman.
They are generally good friends, because it is their interest
to be so, and it is to be hoped that their friendship will
exist forever. They are eminently worthy of each other's
love. They should forget the strifes of the past, and wisely
and nobly cherish and cultivate a fraternal feeling. *Esto
perpetua!*

THE END.